Cyber-Physical Security and Privacy in the Electric Smart Grid

Synthesis Lectures on Information Security, Privacy & Trust

Editors
Elisa Bertino, *Purdue University*
Ravi Sandhu, *University of Texas, San Antonio*

The Synthesis Lectures Series on Information Security, Privacy, and Trust publishes 50- to 100-page publications on topics pertaining to all aspects of the theory and practice of Information Security, Privacy, and Trust. The scope largely follows the purview of premier computer security research journals such as ACM Transactions on Information and System Security, IEEE Transactions on Dependable and Secure Computing and Journal of Cryptology, and premier research conferences, such as ACM CCS, ACM SACMAT, ACM AsiaCCS, ACM CODASPY, IEEE Security and Privacy, IEEE Computer Security Foundations, ACSAC, ESORICS, Crypto, EuroCrypt and AsiaCrypt. In addition to the research topics typically covered in such journals and conferences, the series also solicits lectures on legal, policy, social, business, and economic issues addressed to a technical audience of scientists and engineers. Lectures on significant industry developments by leading practitioners are also solicited.

Cyber-Physical Security and Privacy in the Electric Smart Grid
Bruce McMillin and Thomas Roth
2017

Blocks and Chains: Introduction to Bitcoin, Cryptocurrencies, and Their Consensus Mechanisms
Aljosha Judmayer, Nicholas Stifter, Katharina Krombholz, and Edgar Weippl
2017

Digital Forensic Science: Issues, Methods, and Challenges
Vassil Roussev
2016

Differential Privacy: From Theory to Practice
Ninghui Li, Min Lyu, Dong Su, and Weining Yang
2016

Cyber-Physical Security and Privacy in the Electric Smart Grid

Bruce McMillin and Thomas Roth

ISBN: 978-3-031-01225-9   paperback
ISBN: 978-3-031-02353-8   ebook

DOI 10.1007/978-3-031-02353-8

A Publication in the Morgan & Claypool Publishers series
SYNTHESIS LECTURES ON INFORMATION SECURITY, PRIVACY & TRUST

Lecture #21
Series Editors: Elisa Bertino, *Purdue University*
                Ravi Sandhu, *University of Texas, San Antonio*
Series ISSN
Print 1945-9742   Electronic 1945-9750

Cyber-Physical Security and Privacy in the Electric Smart Grid

Bruce McMillin
Missouri University of Science and Technology

Thomas Roth
National Institute of Standards and Technology

SYNTHESIS LECTURES ON INFORMATION SECURITY, PRIVACY & TRUST #21

ABSTRACT

This book focuses on the combined cyber and physical security issues in advanced electric smart grids. Existing standards are compared with classical results and the security and privacy principles of current practice are illustrated. The book paints a way for future development of advanced smart grids that operated in a peer-to-peer fashion, thus requiring a different security model. Future defenses are proposed that include information flow analysis and attestation systems that rely on fundamental physical properties of the smart grid system.

KEYWORDS

smart grid, security, privacy, cyber-physical, standards

Contents

Preface

A few years ago, the first author was in a research meeting with power engineers looking at building a complex power system testbed for studying dynamics. What about "security?" and the knowing response around the room was "of course it's secure, at long it's not overstressed." Funny response. After some more discussion, it became apparent power system security is a different concept than cyber security, the former being a measure of the system's operation [20][1] (what a computer scientist might refer to as safe and live). "No, what if somebody reads the voltage and power settings?" "Who cares," was the response. And so, with this thought in mind, we begin this book.

The work described herein represents a view developed over the last 17 years of working in what is now known as the "smart grid," both for transmission (high voltage over long distances between electric substations) and distribution (lesser voltage with delivery to customers from a substation). The national laboratories that work in the Department of Energy's mission, national and international standards bodies, experimentation in the research lab for both transmission and distribution have all helped to begin to frame the cyber aspects of electric power security. The cyber aspects become more intertwined with the electric power system, so much so that cyber-physical security seems an appropriate moniker. As this book will uncover, cyber processing and communications system can both help and hinder the resiliency of a power system. The power system still retains some inherent resiliency and its state of operation can provide assistance in its protection from attack.

Bruce McMillin and Thomas Roth
July 2017

---

[1]"Power system security is the ability to maintain the flow of electricity from the generators to the customers, especially under disturbed conditions."

CHAPTER 1

The Smart Grid as a Cyber-Physical System

A cyber-physical system (CPS) integrates a physical infrastructure with cyber computation for improved performance and reliability. The US National Science Foundation established a CPS funding program [1] in the mid-2000s and the National Institute of Standards and Technology established a public working group in 2014 on defining a framework for CPS [10]. Application areas include water distribution, transportation, the electric power grid, chemical process plants, manufacturing, aviation, and medical devices. While control can be centralized, most CPSs are distributed systems in which several cyber processes cooperate to control a set of physical resources. An individual process does not have the complete system state, and must communicate over some network to share information with its peers. It is vital that processes share accurate state information to ensure that the distributed system makes the correct control decisions. Failure in a CPS can result in physical consequences such as damage to the machines or harm to the humans involved in the system operation.

1.1 SMART GRID ARCHITECTURES

The term smart grid can refer to several different types of systems. The most basic smart grid primarily consists of the advanced metering infrastructure (AMI). More advanced smart grids include microgrids, locally generated and consumed power, potentially with energy storage [33], a full distributed distribution systems [46] controlling smart transformers, and transmission level systems that collect data through phasor measurement units (PMUs) and coordinate flow of power and voltage through large-scale electronics devices.

1.1.1 ADVANCED METERING INFRASTRUCTURE

AMI consists of remote electric meter reading over a communications network and limited control of devices or home appliances as in demand side management (DSM). It can potentially measure and control local energy generation and storage and regulate interactions with plug in electric vehicles. It communicates with the electric utility for billing and energy usage reporting and receives control signals for DSM activities such as turning on/off heavy usage appliances (such as air conditioners and water heaters) during periods of high electric usage.

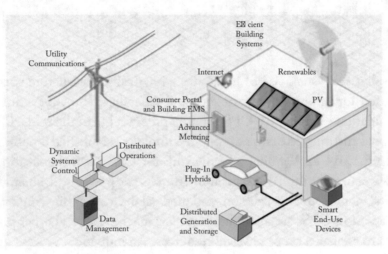

Source: Electric Power Research Institute

Figure 1.1: Concept of the advanced metering infrastructure. Each home has local generation and storage and communicates with an electric utility for pricing signals and operational issues. (Source: Electric Power Research Institute. With Permision.)

1.1.2 MICROGRID ARCHITECTURE

A microgrid is a localized grouping of energy resources including distributed generation, both fossil fuel and renewable (photovoltaic or wind), with an associated Supervisory Control and Data Acquisition (SCADA)(see Section 2.1) that manages the microgrid either synchronous with an existing utility grid, or operating in an islanded mode. Often, energy storage is included (batteries, flywheels) so that the system may operate for limited periods of time without generation. Reasons for using a microgrid can be for improved resilience in the face of generation losses, standalone systems in military forward operating bases, and completely renewable energy architectures.

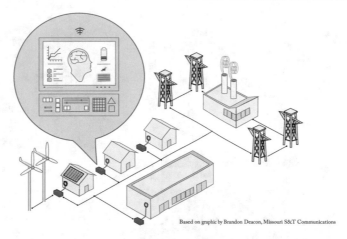

Based on graphic by Brandon Deacon, Missouri S&T Communications

Figure 1.2: Microgrid architecture in which each house contains a home automation network (HAN) for monitoring energy usage. Each house is connected to a SCADA control system (see Section 2.1) that allocates power to the microgrid (or sells it back to the electric utility). (Based on graphic by Brandon Deacon, Missouri S&T Communications.)

1.1.3   FULLY DISTRIBUTED SMART GRID

Moving away from centralized control through peer-to-peer system operation is an Internet of Things concept (IoT), or an energy internet. The Future Renewable Electric Energy Delivery and Management (FREEDM) system [17, 46] is a ten-year U.S. National Science Foundation (NSF) project that forms an example of an energy internet. Each SST negotiates with peer SSTs through a cyber broker architecture to provide distributed energy management, power balancing, and voltage stability support (Figure 1.3). The cyber negotiation results in settings of the power electronics to transfer power either to or from a shared distribution bus. Ideally such a system can operate in grid-connected mode or in islanded mode where it is completely self sufficient.

As another example, IPERC corporation's Gridmaster® [3] is a commercial distributed product that was used to create the SPIDERS microgrid system for U.S. Department of Defense systems. It uses dynamic group management and distributed reconfiguration.

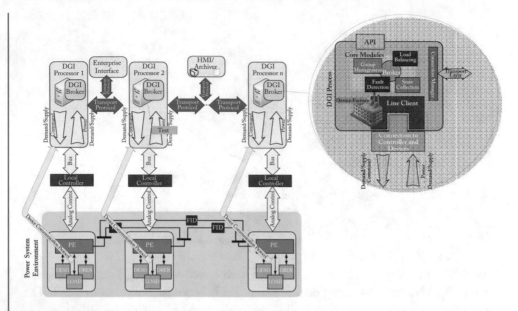

Figure 1.3: The FREEDM system of fully distributed smart grid. It is organized into an intelligent energy management system that coordinates distributed renewable energy resource (DRER), distributed energy storage devices (DESD), and LOADs through a distributed grid intelligence (DGI) that coordinates power electronics (PE) devices for transactive energy management and reactive power support.

1.1.4   TRANSMISSION GRID

The bulk transmission grid is one of the most complicated human-engineered systems, short of the Internet. It has evolved over 100 years from vertically integrated electric utilities to interconnected power systems that can buy and sell power from each others (Figure 1.4). Generation of power comes from traditional sources such as coal, nuclear, or hydro and may include renewable resources such as wind or solar. Power is consumed by loads connected to distribution systems. Transmission systems carry the power from generation to substations which deliver the power through distribution systems (such as those listed above). Historically, control of the transmission system is limited to opening or closing relays, turning on or off generators, and, in the worst case, disconnecting loads. These commands come a central control center owned by an electric utility.

More modern power systems include power electronics elements such as Flexible AC Transmission (FACTS) devices that can add voltage support (STATCOM[1]) or can modify electric power flows (UPFC[2]) under cyber control from the utility.

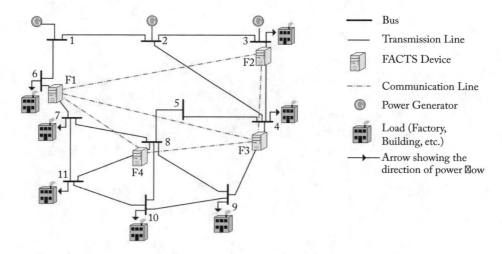

Figure 1.4: Conceptual diagram of an electric power transmission system showing generators (coal, nuclear, wind) serving loads, potentially supported by advanced power electronics devices such as FACTS.

[1]A Static Synchronous Compensator is a shunt or parallel device.
[2]Unified Power Flow Controller that contains both series and shut elements.

CHAPTER 2

The Basics of Cyber-Physical Security

Confidentiality, integrity, and availability (CIA) form the classic triad of cyber security [4]. Essentially, confidentiality is the aspect where an unauthorized entity does not gain access to some protected information; entities and techniques such as encryption of data and firewalls attempt to preserve confidentiality. Integrity preserves the systems's information and resources from disruption; again, firewalls and authentication restrict access to the system's information to reduce the possibility of disruption. Availability ensures that access to information, services, and resources is not prevented.

Within cyber-physical security, CIA is refined. In current practice, availability is often seen as more importance followed by integrity and confidentiality, but this is changing as all begin to take on equal priorities. Confidentiality can take on several aspects, but the goal is always the same, leaving a party in doubt about what is being observed. The first is protecting control signals from disclosure, the idea being that if an attacker can ascertain control signals, the attacker can understand more about the state of the system. From a consumer of view, monitoring of electrical usage can present privacy issues, potentially leaking electric usage down to the appliance level. Integrity violation ultimately results in unauthorized modification of the electric power system, either by destabilizing its operation, or by exploiting it, economically. This can be done by direct manipulation of control signals by an attacker, or by spoofing control readings, leading the power system control to make incorrect decisions [72]. Availability violation, like integrity, changes the electric power system to make it unavailable to the consumer (through either blackouts or through changing the power quality).

The CIA triad are Security Policies, an expression of what is desired to hold from a security standpoint. It is key for system designers, users, and standards agencies to be able to express what properties are desired. These can include time of system availability, prevention of disruption, what information must be kept confidential, and from whom, and what information must be kept private. Security Mechanisms, by contrast, enforce the security policies and are designed and implemented by the system's designers.

2.1   A LOOK AT THE HISTORY OF SCADA SYSTEMS AND SECURITY

Most current systems are controlled by supervisory control and data acquisition (SCADA) systems that control physical devices and acquire readings of physical resources. The earliest SCADA systems were really telemetry monitoring systems, measuring power flow and voltage at instrumented points of the power grid as well as device statuses. Networking, as such, could be over telephone lines or could be manual reports from the field. These measurements are fed into a state estimation algorithm to generate the complete system state, which analysts at the control center use to monitor for problems and make corrective actions. Historically, control center operations within an electric utility were limited to opening or closing switches on power lines to enable or disable connections with a power distribution network and connect or disconnect substations or generators through switch settings. Power system operators relied on an intuitive feel for how to keep the power grid secure and avoid moving into unstable states. Some of the earliest uses of digital control for power systems are in the mid-sixties [24, 35] which were programs to calculate switching settings for operator reference through offline calculations. These moved on to logic-adaptive control [25] in which line and frequency security are monitored and action is taken to correct generation. A simplified SCADA system is shown in Figure 2.1 in which the SCADA system provides switch settings (actuators) through Remote Terminal Units (RTUs) and collects data from sensors attached to the RTUs. The key point is that switch settings can be beneficial or deleterious to secure power system operation.

The National Academies report on terrorism [8] identified some of the earliest security concerns were due to sabotage during war. Power plant security focused more on physical intrusion detection and mitigation [23]. These early views permeate a perimeter defense posture. One early Department of Energy report, "21 Steps to Improve Cyber Security of SCADA Networks" [50], enumerates mostly operational steps of risk assessment, people management, iden-

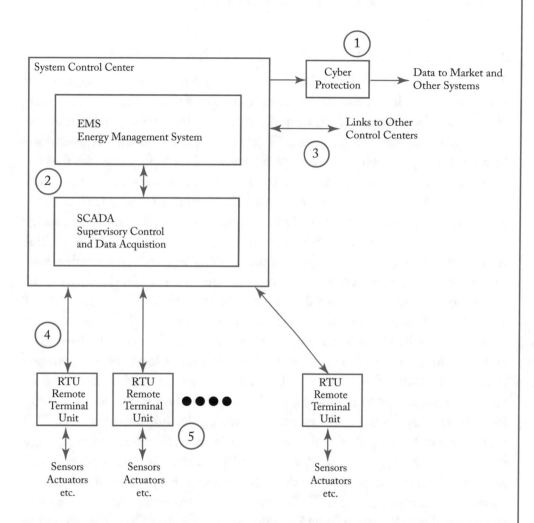

Figure 2.1: Simplified SCADA control system [8]. The numbers refer to points of vulnerability. The cyber protection, in this model, consists of mechanisms such as firewalls to restrict access to sensitive information and prevent malicious control signals from reaching the control system.

tifying connections, and auditing. The Industrial Control Systems Cyber Emergency Response Team(ICS-CERT) [38] maintains a list of numerous standards and practices [63] and provides a comparison indicating that SCADA-specific standards are more focused on technical perimeter countermeasures.

2.1.1   CLASSIC MODELS OF SECURITY: BLP AND BIBA

The Bell-La Padula model (BLP) [18] forms the basis for what most would consider as security. It consists of actors and objects that are arranged into levels such as Top Secret, Secret, Confidential, and Unclassified, and also allows for categories of security clearances. Objects (such as documents) are described by a level, category pair and actors have a level and multiple categories that the actor can access. An actor can read down in security levels or write up in security levels to other actors or to objects, essentially forming a security lattice. However, an actor cannot write down or read up in security. The goal is to prevent information at a higher security level from flowing to a lower security level. This is quite clearly inspired by a military security policy in which commanders have higher security clearances than do troops on the ground. On the surface, the model appears quite good, but there's a problem: How does a commander give commands to their troops as such an action would violate the no write down principle? The BLP model allows for an actor to lower their security level to be able to communicate with an actor or object at a lower level. What about potential information flows, though? The actor that has lowered its security level must be trusted not to divulge higher level information to the lower security level, essentially defeating the entire process. A naive implementation of BLP is showing in Figure 2.2. Within the context of an electric power system, there are two primary types of processes: control processes and business enterprise activities. Using BLP it becomes difficult to arrange a System Control Center (level 2) with respect to the RTUs (level 3) and sensors/actuators (level 4) of the physical power system (level 5). If the System Control Center is at a higher security level than the RTUs/sensors and the power system (which seems reasonable) how does it send commands to the power system? If the situation is reversed and the RTUs/sensors and the power system is at a higher security level, how does the power system send status readings to the System Control Center or to the system operator? As such, while BLP is conceptually easy to understand, its implementation is not a good fit. Implementation of BLP, how-

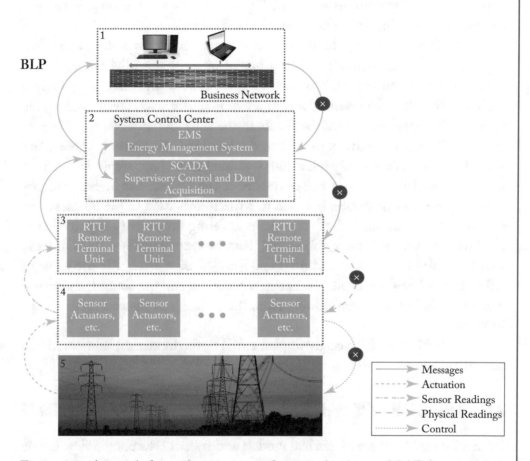

Figure 2.2: A straightforward assignment of security levels to a SCADA system under the Bell-La Padula model. Information flows and messages are indicated by green arrows and prohibited information flows are shown with an "X". The "no write down" aspect of BLP prevents the control center in level 2 from controlling the RTUs in level 3 and prevents the RTUs from controlling the actuators in level 4 and prevents the actuators from controlling the power system in level 5.

ever, produces a valuable configuration of a modern electric utility, essentially that the business enterprise of a utility cannot write down into the control system, if the control system is placed at a lower security level, thus preventing a potential virus that has compromised the business enterprise from impacting with the control system, as shown in Figure 2.3. The reasons for this become clearer when looking at the next model, the Biba model.

The Biba mode [18] looks at security from another approach, one of integrity. By contrast with the military model of BLP, the Biba model can be considered as a commercial model. Like BLP, Biba is organized into levels, a high integrity level can write down to a low integrity level, but it cannot read from the lower integrity level. To do so, in the Biba low water mark, policy reduces the integrity of the high level to the low level. As I tell my classes, "it's sort of like watching reality television; watching something stupid lowers your intelligence." In an electric power system, if the control has higher integrity than the business processes, it is free to write information to the business, but cannot accept commands from it without lowering its integrity level to that of the business. On reflection, this model describes actual utility operation fairly well for centrally-administered AMI and Transmission system. It also explains why a firewall exists between the business processes and the control, and that it prevents information from flowing from the business to the control as shown in Figure 2.4.

Both BLP and Biba can be implemented through extensive computational security mechanisms to enforce their policies.

2.2   SECURITY PARTITIONS IN THE SMART GRID

Both Biba and BLP are hierarchial models and restrict information flow in one direction or the other. When just two levels of control and business are considered, as above, the model can be made to work. If we add in the customer, however, in an AMI environment, what security or integrity level do they get assigned? Are they lower security than the business, higher security than the business? Where do the electric meters fit—are they at a lower security level than control? The lower security level doesn't work if the System Control Center wants to send commands to the meter as in DSM. If the meter is at a higher security level, then it cannot send its readings to the control. For integrity, we see the same problems. As such, the meters have to be at the same security level

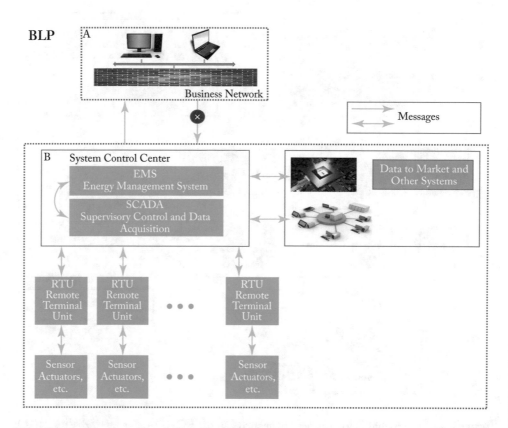

Figure 2.3: A reasonable assignment of security in the SCADA system under the Bell-La Padula model. Information flows and messages are indicated by green arrows and prohibited information flows are shown with an "X". This picture illustrates that it is more important to protect the control system from the business than the business from the control system. BLP also requires that all other control systems are in the same security level, otherwise they cannot share information.

BIBA

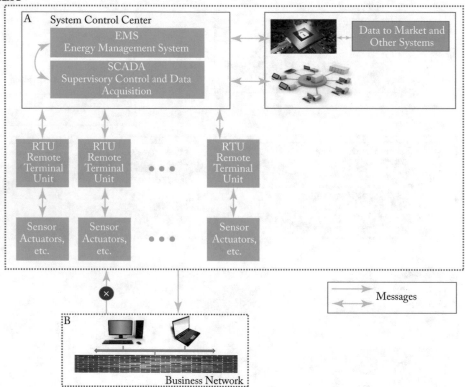

Figure 2.4: A reasonable assignment of security in the SCADA system under the BIBA model. Information flows and messages are indicated by green arrows and prohibited information flows are shown with an "X". This picture illustrates that the integrity of the control system is higher than that of the business network. As with BLP, BIBA also requires that all other control systems are in the same security level, otherwise they cannot share information.

as the control. This uncovers a duality present in electric power systems, and in cyber-physical systems, in general. In reality, some of CIA are bidirectional. Confidentiality, for instance, contains bidirectional information flow. In the one aspect, confidentiality is concerned with the flow of information from the control center to the outside world. On the other aspect, spoofing disrupts the flow of information into the control center. Both directions leave one party in doubt about what is being observed. Integrity attacks can be detected if the doubt is removed.

Consider the case of Stuxnet, which resulted in the widespread installation of malware into Siemens programmable logic controllers (PLCs) [27]. The controllers infected by Stuxnet attempted to damage centrifuges by causing malicious changes to their rotor speeds. At the same time, Stuxnet sent false state reports which indicated normal rotor speeds back to human operators. One of Stuxnet's goals was for the false state information to trick the operators into making the wrong control decision, namely, keeping the centrifuges running. The Stuxnet attack was able to succeed because there was only one information and control path, once that was compromised the Stuxnet worm left the System Control Center in doubt regarding the information it was receiving. In a metering environment, spoofed meter readings could appear perfectly normal to the control system, but be incorrect (such as overreporting or underreporting electric load). Additional information is needed to locate such attacks such as in [52] which uses the physics of the system to inject high-frequency signals into an electric grid to detect faulty nodes by finding a mismatch between expected and measured impedances.

Early cybersecurity research formalized the model of how information flow can be disrupted through the model of nondeducbility [66]. Consider two partitions called left and right.[1] Let a world w be a state of the system. Then define an information function $f_1(w)$ to be all of the events in the left partition that led to the state w, and a second function $f_2(w)$ for all the events in the right partition. An observation z is nondeducible from the point of view of the right partition if:

$$(\forall w \in W)(\exists w' \in W : f_1(w) = f_1(w') \wedge f_2(w') = z \wedge w \neq w'). \qquad (2.1)$$

---

[1]These partitions could be called high and low, or low and high, it doesn't make any difference. As such, the model can describe bidirectional information flow.

Equation (2.1) is satisfied if all possible left command sequences $f_1(w)$ can produce the same observation z in the right partition using the information function $f_2()$. Put more simply, if z is the same observation no matter what commands are executed, an observer in the right partition can never deduce what happened in the left partition. Nondeducibility models the Stuxnet attack; the left partition is the PLC controller and the right partition is the System Control Center. All readings, z, that the System Control Center received were consistent with any possible correct operating mode of the centrifuges—the attack was nondeducibly secure [36].

This may appear as a strange result, the notion that an attack is somehow secure. However, not being able to deduce an attack, makes it confidential, which leads to an integrity violation. Not all nondeducible results are bad, however, nondeducibility for system confidentiality is a good thing; it can protect control signals from disclosure and preserve personal privacy in an electric smart grid by leaving an attacked in doubt as to what they are observing.

A modern smart grid inherently has multiple security domains as shown in Figure 2.5. The multiple security domain nondeducibiity model (MSDND) [37] describes the ability of an attacker or defender to observe if a system state is true or false. For example, in Figure 2.5, someone inside a house can tell if power is available or not, but cannot tell if power is available in another house. If they can see the Leader Board, then they can tell power usage, but not how the power is used. The Governance can see all power flows, but still cannot look inside an individual house. An attacker might be able to create an intrusion a disrupt the power to one house, as in Stuxnet, but not to multiple houses without being detected. This is a potentially powerful model that allows quantification of both a system's vulnerability to integrity attacks and resilience to confidentiality attacks.

Another, older, model than nondeducibility is noninterference [30] which simply states the following. Given a system that contains two partitions, left and right, and a trace, z resulting from executing the system, then the system is nonintererence secure if an observer cannot distinguish if any events in the left have occurred. If we think about a System Control Center in the left partition and an observer in the right partition, for such a system to be noninterference secure requires that no actions in the left partition ever cause something to be observed in the right partition. Clearly, no electric power system could function

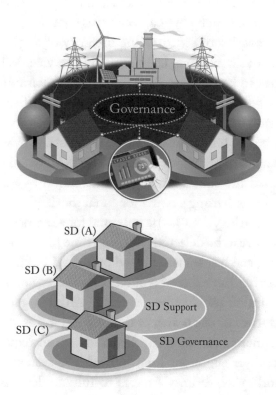

Figure 2.5: (a) A modern neighborhood in which information and power is shared and displayed via an electronic Leader Board. (b) Overlapping security domains with SD(A), SD(B), SD(C) as individual houses, SD Support as the shared power infrastructure, and SD Governance that oversees all the houses, but not inside the houses.

if it were noninterference secure, it would never be able to change the physical system.

2.3   VULNERABILITY ASSESSMENTS OF POWER SYSTEMS

Vulnerability assessment of a power system is, in many ways, easier than that of a purely cyber system, if cyber-physical security is consider together, rather than as a separate cyber overlay of security. The integrity of a cyber-physical power system has a rather basic measure, keep providing service. While a lot of valuable work continues to be done on detecting unusual communication patterns within a control system [21], another body of work quantifies the actual impact of a security intrusion on the physical infrastructure being managed [68]; if the power system will be put into an unsafe state, as measured by voltage stability or available transfer capacity metrics then the impact is high and should mitigated. This can be extended the substation's cyber interaction by examining network events. If events such as "wrong passwd" or "unauthorized file change" followed by a physical device setting, there is the potential for a temporal anomaly against the power system that can be detected [34]. The time to compromise the system, using such methods, can be estimated based on the skill of the attacker [75]. By comparison, measuring the effect of a purely cyber intrusion can be more difficult; how could a similar measure be developed within a game or a social network? The ground truth of the health of the physical infrastructure makes CPS vulnerability assessment feasible, if not easier. To do so requires a close cooperation of electric power engineers, knowledgeable in system dynamics, control system experts, and cyber security experts to fully understand cyber-physical security.

The cyber aspect of the electric smart grid is often quoted as adding additional resiliency and functionality to an electric power system. However, the impact that a malfunctioning or compromised control system can have on the electric grid can be significant. In one study, coordinated UPFC FACTS devices balance power through a distributed maximum flow algorithm to change real power flows to prevent cascading failures. Their operation was simulated in a stressed IEEE 118 bus model designed to simulate a situation similar to that of the 2003 Northeast blackout in which tripping of an overloaded, but small capacity, power line induced a cascading failure. When operating properly, the

FACTS devices coordinate to route power away from overloaded transmission lines to less loaded lines, preventing line trips. Injecting cyber faults into the FACTS device's controllers increased the number of cascading failures since the resulting incorrect FACTS settings either did not react to the overload, or set the power lines to incorrect power flow settings. Essentially, the switch settings from improper cyber control can reduce the resiliency of the power grid [28]. This did not happen in all cases, however; the power grid retains a good deal of resilience to poor cyber settings. [72] observed similar aspects for a distribution grid's voltage control system. It introduces a combined cyber-physical model with specific information flows that can be disrupted, delayed, or modified. The performance of the voltage control system under various attacks was assessed with respect to the voltage in the power system. For this particular algorithm, the power system was inherently resilient to a number of cyber failures and delays while others caused failure of the system. It's not the connection or disconnection of a communications network that induces failures, it's the result of message or computer modification that produces poor switch settings that lead to failure.

This begs the question "How does an attacker know when or how to attack?" In keeping with NERC CIP requirements [12], protection of control settings from outside observation is required. Certainly if an attacker is able to log into the system, they can observe it and can tell where to launch the attack, whether it be disrupting message communication to prevent a switch setting from occurring or modifying a message or a control algorithm to produce the wrong switch setting. But what if all paths are blocked for the attacker to enter the system and all messages are perfectly encrypted? The challenge is that information still flows out of the system through the switching actions. In the cascading failure example, above, if an attacker can determine that something is mitigating a potential failure (FACTS devices) and the attacker knows the algorithm being used (max flow), then by observing the individual power line changes, the attacker can determine the complete state of the power system and when it is most vulnerable. The next step is to launch a cyber-enabled physical attack on that particular power line the FACTS devices are protecting. Clearly, this system can never be noninterference secure, it will always make a physical change in the power system. If, however, the settings can be made nondeducible [29], then the attacker is left in doubt.

2.3.1 INFORMATION FLOW DISRUPTION

As mentioned in Section 2.2, disruption of information flow to a controller can cause a serious impact on a physical system.

Information flow disruption is not a new problem. The state estimation algorithms in the electric power grid use bad data detection algorithms to detect and remove bad measurements and were proposed in the 1960s [58]. The goal of bad data detection is to determine which measurements obtained from the field have been corrupted due to meter faults, and discard these measurements to prevent a negative impact on the control of the power grid. As in the previous sections, being able to have the state of the power system is critical to being able to detect and mitigate an attack. However, bad data detection was not designed to handle state fabrications due to an intelligent attack, and compromise attacks that bypass bad data detection have been discovered in literature.

There is a large body of work that explores how spoofed readings from power line flows can disrupt information flow and go undetected at a control center. This modern study traces to [45] which characterized how a false data injection attack can make intelligent modifications to the measurements delivered to a SCADA system and fool state estimation into producing an incorrect system state. This is a Stuxnet-like attack where a subset of sensors located at buses in the power grid are compromised and send false state reports back to the control center. The false reports are chosen to be consistent with the physical topology of the grid to pass through state estimation undetected. A false data injection attack chooses falsified measurements that are consistent with the physical topology of the system to bypass traditional bad data detection implementations. A topology attack can falsify switch and breaker signals to trick the bad data detection algorithm into working with the wrong physical topology [41]. Both of these attacks are unobservable in that, from the perspective of state estimation, the measurements are consistent with the perceived physical topology and contain no error.

CHAPTER 3

Defenses

3.1 ATTESTATION THROUGH PHYSICAL PROPERTIES

Attestation is normally associated with ensuring that a particular computing element is meeting its standards, either through static techniques such as memory hashing or dynamic techniques such as comparing byte code [60] and remote assertion checking [59]. Dynamic techniques work by ensuring that system invariants on the code execution are met. These invariants may come from the system specification [55, 69], or, potentially, from synthesis tools, like Daikon. For the attestation to be meaningful, it must be done remotely, that is another process or watchdog independently verifies that a process under scrutiny satisfies its requirements [61]. If the test is done locally, it is possible that the test, itself, is suspect.

Attestation within the context of the power grid adds another dimension [40]. The predominant trend in literature to prevent unobservable attacks is to utilize a piece of physical hardware called a phasor measurement unit (PMU). A PMU utilizes global positioning system (GPS) synchronized clocks to produce high fidelity meter readings of the power system. It has been suggested that PMU deployment can be useful in protection against unobservable by providing a set of trusted measurements to the state estimation algorithm [26]. Research in this direction has explored which buses are most vulnerable through formulation of security indices which quantify how useful each bus is in producing unobservable attacks [57]. PMUs can then be deployed at vulnerable buses to create redundant, trustworthy measurements that can be utilized in state estimation to detect false data injection [19]. However, this approach assumes that PMUs are tamper resistant and cannot be compromised in the same manner as the sensors deployed in the existing power grid.

Besides PMU deployment for redundant measurements, several methods have proposed modified bad data detection algorithms resilient against false state injection. One distributed approach estimates the false data injection alongside the system state and eliminates the attack vector from the state estimation [67]. Another approach proposes a change to the residual function used to detect bad data to include local bus measurements such as voltage and phase angle [65]. Observation of which bus measurements lead to high error terms during state estimation will then isolate the location at which compromises are likely to have occurred. However, all of these approaches retain a centralized power utility that performs the control actions.

Physically unclonable functions (PUFs) [48] are another attempt to ensure that components within the smart grid are: (1) not counterfeit by ensuring that responses in key exchange protocols are unique and (2) ensuring that the device is executing the correct, unmodified, code, by monitoring its output signals and timing. Since no two physical devices, even those of the same design, produce exactly the same physical characteristics, each procedures a unique signature. Ensuring the device is executing the correct code is more difficult, particularly if the attacker has the ability to modify the device's code and/or control algorithms. In this case external analog and digital monitoring is needed [39].

Several implementations of software attestation for smart meters have been proposed [51, 64]. An extension of attestation for the smart grid proposes the use of control signal injection from the centralized SCADA control to challenge meters or controls distributed in the physical system [69]. The response to this challenge could then be fed through a detection algorithm similar to bad data detection to look for compromises.

In more advanced, distributed, versions of the smart grid, control shifts from a centralized control center to distributed intelligence. Through the use of renewable energy resources and local energy storage, the smart grid proposes to manage energy resources on a peer-to-peer basis at the residential level. It has been shown that false data injection attacks in the smart grid impact both the cost of energy and the outage ratio for households [44]. One challenge of the future smart grid will be address how to handle false data detection in a distributed control system. One approach to performing distributed attestation is to use observations of the physical medium to gauge malicious behavior rather than the results of a challenge issued by some tester. Physical attestation is based on the observation that changes in cyber process state affect the physical infrastructure due to the tight coupling between the cyber and physical layers. The physical infrastructure is therefore a high-integrity message channel of information that contains a portion of the cyber process state. With physical attestation, a cyber process uses feedback from the physical system to validate the states of its peers. In essence, physical attestation takes the work done with bad data detection in power grids and implements it as a distributed cyber security mechanism [55].

3.2 ATTESTATION THROUGH REPUTATION

A companion approach to attestation is to consider reputation-based security. Compromised home meters, for example, can indicate some sort of tampering either to hide specific electical usage patterns [73] or to simply avoid billing. The big question becomes, how to establish reputation? [54] posed an interesting sociological history-based approach. Using household income as a metric, what are the expected usage patterns? If they fall outside the norm, then the reputation of the meter decreases. A more engineering approach is taken by [74] by considering misbehaving units within an energy management algorithm. Through an iterative approach in which all generators communicate each others values, generators are dispatched within a power distribution system to minimize overall cost. If a generator provides inconsistent or an out-of-bound setting, then it can drive the system to instability. As a generator performs more incorrect values, its reputation decreases and its impact on the incremental cost is lessened. The algorithm is able to detect correct or incorrect operation by ensuring that the resulting computing matches the generation with the load. The threat model of using inconsistent data is similar to that of reducing inconsistency through Byzantine Agreement [42] and there is potential to explore these two concepts, together.

3.3 STATISTICAL CONTROL APPROACHES

Between Attestation and Reputation are approaches that predetermine the effect on a physical system from a control setting. [56] examines the payload of a control setting delivered by a network—if it is consistent the normalcy of a control setting, it is allowed, otherwise it is discarded. The work of [22] goes on to investigate different categories of attacks within dynamic control system models of the physical system.

CHAPTER 4

Attack Motivation

NIST 7628 6.2.1 and [8] enumerate attackers as hackers, disgruntled employees, agents of industrial espionage, and terrorists with both limited and significant capabilities, and power market participants looking for an economic advantage. Inadvertent compromises of the information infrastructure due to user errors, equipment failures, and natural disasters can also be considered as attacks.

The Ukraine power system attack was carried about by another nation to specifically disrupt electric power delivery [43]. From an economic perspective, an attacker would be motivated to perform false data injection due to its ability to impact prices in the electric energy market which can lead to economic gain [71]. However, a recent state survey of electric and water utilities using the NIST 800-030 Guide for Conducting Risk Assessments [7] indicated that the attack motivation was not always clear, nor were the risks or likelihood of attack [14]. NIST has called for an increasing situational awareness within the electric utilities [16].

CHAPTER 5

Privacy

5.1 NILM

Section 2.2 has discussed the information leakage inherent in a Smart Grid by characterizing control setting leakage of power electronics devices through an observable physical response. The issue is more pervasive than this; within a home environment, individual appliances also produce a signature that can be observed both from meter readings and directly on the power line entering the residence. This has become the subject the emerging area of non intrusive load monitoring (NILM). No instrumentation of individual appliances is necessary. There are some positive aspects to this. Within a HAN, a consumer can monitor their individual appliance usage in an effort to conserve energy [70]. In building automation systems, malfunctioning units may be identified [62]. Electric utilities have interest in developing usage profiles of their customers [32]. In looking at Figure 5.1, a privacy issue becomes clear. If an external observer can see when appliances are on or off, it tells not only when someone is home, but what their personal habits are. NIST 7628 6.2.1 was primarily concerned with electric utilities selling usage data to third parties and with law enforcement attempting to establish activities within the home. NILM methods work by modeling each potential individual appliance's power or energy transitions (on/off/power change) [47] within the home. When the appliances are in operation together, the combination cannot be easily extracted. Hidden Markov models [73] are attractive as they are able to disaggregate these individual models from the combined power usage.

Since the individual appliance signatures cannot be hidden from observation, their behavior is not noninterference secure. Can they be made nondeducibly secure since to do so would be to mask one appliance usage with another appliance? Such a technique is load masking [49] in which local energy storage can be used instead of a grid connection to obfuscate energy usage by a particular appliance.

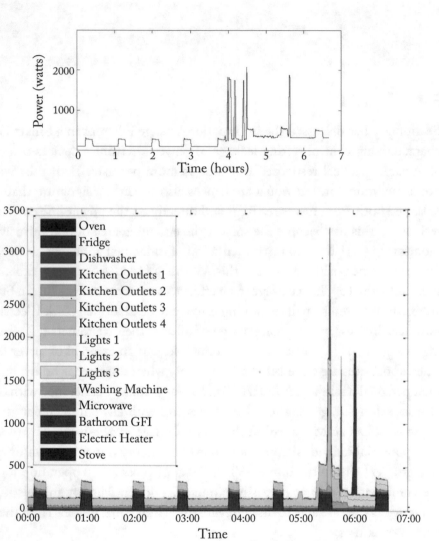

Figure 5.1: Non intrusive load monitoring of appliances [11].

5.2   QUANTIFYING THE HUMAN ELEMENT

How humans will react to potential privacy concerns within a smart grid is an embryonic area of study, requiring close interaction among the computer and social sciences and electrical engineering. Questions such as "what will people give up in terms of privacy for economic benefit, for social benefit, or for environmental benefit" require a deep understanding of human behavior in a future environment. Current population survey methods fall short as they cannot place themselves within these future environments. Some psychological models, such as Communications Privacy Management (CPM) [53], have the potential to quantify privacy concerns through discussion of boundaries and when those boundaries are violated. There is the potential for significant contributions to be made in this area.

CHAPTER 6

Standards

Standards for cybersecurity for electric power systems have evolved from the earlier days in which information technology services were seen as a supporting role, but rarely operational. The first widely attributed instance of cyber contributing to a power system failure was during the August 2003 blackout [5] where delayed SCADA readings due to failed computers caused a loss of operator situational awareness that contributed to the widespread blackout in the northeast U.S. The NERC and NIST standards have looked at threats to the evolving cyber infrastructure from a perimeter defense and management standpoint, consistent with centralized operational procedures practiced by the electric utilities. The SGIP looks beyond centralized control and begins to consider threats that go beyond perimeter defenses.

6.1 NERC

The North American Electric Reliability Corporation (NERC) is a regulatory authority that develops and enforces Reliability Standards for the Bulk Electric System (BES). It is overseen by the Federal Energy Regulatory Commission (FERC) in the United States and governmental authorities in Canada. The standards govern a wide range of BES operation grounded in a risk-based approach. Systems governed by NERC standards are classified into high, medium, or low impact based on the amount of power handled by each classification.

6.1.1 NERC CIP

The critical infrastructure protection (CIP) standards govern three primary areas of physical security, cyber security, and personnel/change management. The primary approach taken is one of perimeter security. In the cyber world this follows the analog of physical perimeter security and extends the concept to firewalls and control of network access from the outside of the system. There has been an evolution of these standards beginning with critical cyber asset protection, and more recently evolving into BES Cyber Systems, reflecting the tighter integration of the cyber with the electric system. The distinction of perimeter security continues to dominate. Standard CIP-003-6, in particular, regulates communication into or out of a low-impact BES system, consistent with the BIBA model of integrity (Figure 6.1). Note that the firewall shown between the BES Asset boundary and the business processes prevents access from the business processes to the BES Asset boundary, in other words, relative to the BES, the business processes have less integrity. CIP-005-5 specifically relates high and lower impact systems by requiring that each high impact system with an electronic access point have an electronic security perimeter and that if it interacts with any other protected domain that they all correspond to a high-water mark (again a BIBA policy term). CIP-003-6 goes on to particularly exclude "point-to-point communications between intelligent electronic devices that use routable communication protocols for time-sensitive protection or control functions," essentially considering communication within the protected domain as secured by other means as in the BIBA and BLP models of SCADA security in Section 2.1.1. Figure 6.2 provides a summary evolution of these standards.

6.2 SGIP AND NIST

The Smart Grid Interoperability Panel (SGIP) works to bring public and private stakeholders in the electric grid's design and operation together to increase interoperability. Since the electric grid still largely built with legacy and proprietary technology, it is not completely interoperable. The goal of the SGIP is to interlink proprietary technologies together from the aspects of IoT and systems integration building in cybersecurity. While not explicitly stated, many of the products of the SGIP have strong cyber-physical aspects.

6.2.1 NISTIR 7628

SGIP and NIST partnered in 2009 through NIST's Cyber Security Working Group (CSWG) to develop Security and Privacy in the Smart grid. This produced a series of three volumes [11] of a (1) a Smart Grid Cybersecurity Strategy, (2) Privacy and Security, and (3) Supportive Analyses. It is a rather daunting read; [31] does an effective job of consolidating the 46 actors over 7 domains (Figure 6.3) with the 130 logical interactions represented in the reports. A user's guide [6] provides a process for identifying risks and mapping them to 7628. Classic security aspects such as key management and cryptography are re-

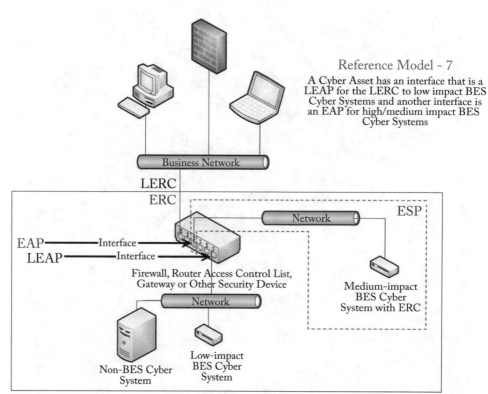

Reference Model - 7

A Cyber Asset has an interface that is a LEAP for the LERC to low impact BES Cyber Systems and another interface is an EAP for high/medium impact BES Cyber Systems

Figure 6.1: A NERC CIP-003-6 Low Impact model showing the BES Asset Boundary as a Security Domain firewalled from the business network [12]. The terms used in the figure are (Low) Impact BES Cyber System Electronic Access Points (L)EAPs and (Low) Impact External Routable Connectivity (L)ERC).

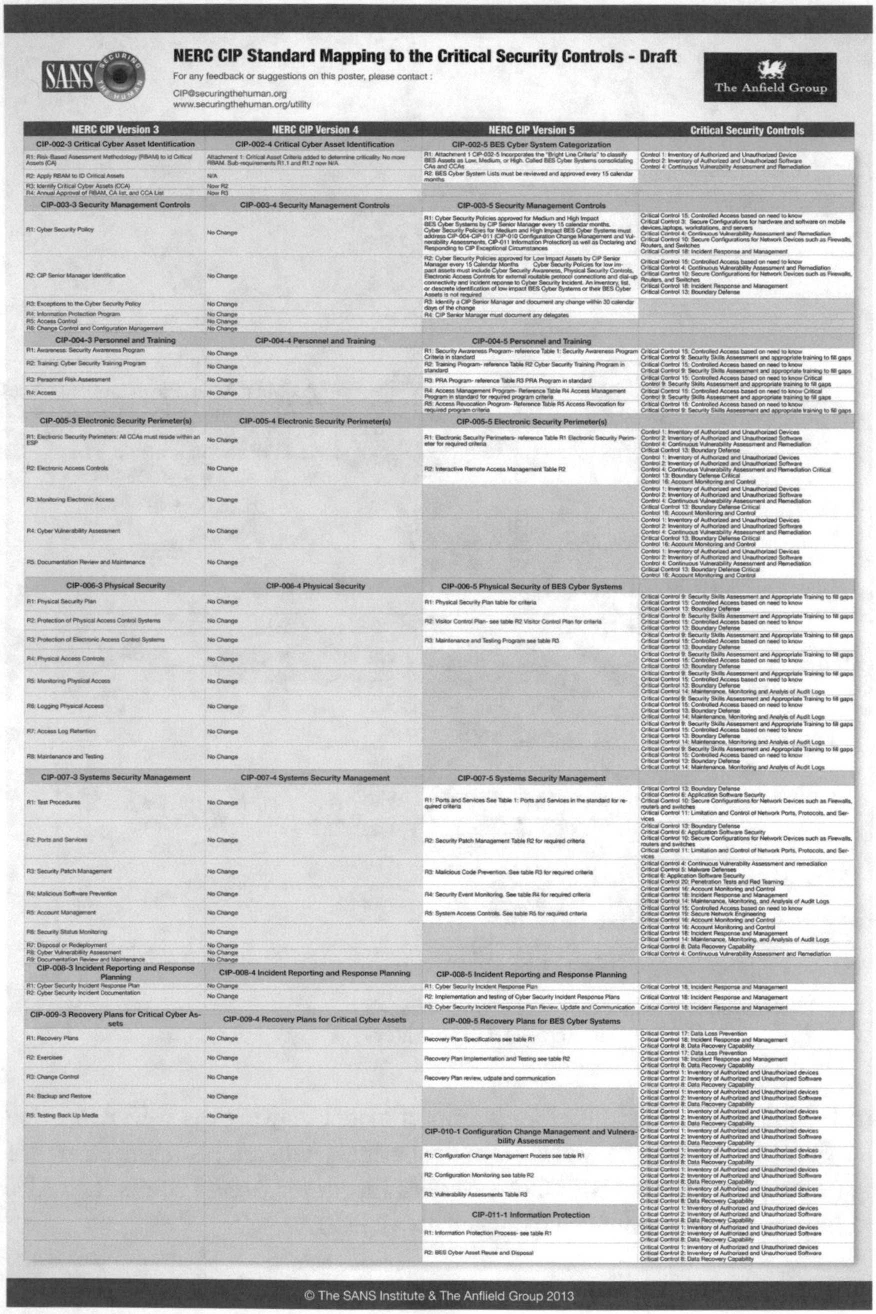

NERC CIP Standard Mapping to the Critical Security Controls - Draft

For any feedback or suggestions on this poster, please contact :

CIP@securingthehuman.org
www.securingthehuman.org/utility

NERC CIP Version 3	NERC CIP Version 4	NERC CIP Version 5	Critical Security Controls
CIP-002-3 Critical Cyber Asset Identification	**CIP-002-4 Critical Cyber Asset Identification**	**CIP-002-5 BES Cyber System Categorization**	
R1: Risk-Based Assessment Methodology (RBAM) to id Critical Assets (CA)	Attachment 1: Critical Asset Criteria added to determine criticality. No more RBAM. Sub-requirements R1.1 and R1.2 now N/A	R1: Attachment 1 CIP-002-5 incorporates the "Bright Line Criteria" to classify BES Assets as Low, Medium, or High. Called BES Cyber Systems consolidating CAs and CCAs	Control 1: Inventory of Authorized and Unauthorized Device Control 2: Inventory of Authorized and Unauthorized Software Control 4: Continuous Vulnerability Assessment and Remediation
R2: Apply RBAM to ID Critical Assets	N/A	R2: BES Cyber System Lists must be reviewed and approved every 15 calendar months	
R3: Identify Critical Cyber Assets (CCA)	Now R2		
R4: Annual Approval of RBAM, CA list, and CCA List	Now R3		
CIP-003-3 Security Management Controls	**CIP-003-4 Security Management Controls**	**CIP-003-5 Security Management Controls**	
R1: Cyber Security Policy	No Change	R1: Cyber Security Policies approved for Medium and High Impact BES Cyber Systems by CIP Senior Manager every 15 calendar months. Cyber Security Policies for Medium and High Impact BES Cyber Systems must address CIP-004-CIP-011 (CIP-010 Configuration Change Management and Vulnerability Assessments, CIP-011 Information Protection) as well as Declaring and Responding to CIP Exceptional Circumstances	Critical Control 15: Controlled Access based on need to know Critical Control 3: Secure Configurations for hardware and software on mobile devices,laptops, workstations, and servers Critical Control 4: Continuous Vulnerability Assessment and Remediation Critical Control 10: Secure Configurations for Network Devices such as Firewalls, Routers, and Switches Critical Control 18: Incident Response and Management
R2: CIP Senior Manager Identification	No Change	R2: Cyber Security Policies approved for Low Impact Assets by CIP Senior Manager every 15 Calendar Months Cyber Security Policies for low impact assets must include Cyber Security Awareness, Physical Security Controls, Electronic Access Controls for external routable protocol connections and dial-up connectivity and incident reponse to Cyber Security Incident. An inventory, list, or descrete identification of low impact BES Cyber Systems or their BES Cyber Assets is not required	Critical Control 15: Controlled Access based on need to know Critical Control 4: Continuous Vulnerability Assessment and Remediation Critical Control 10: Secure Configurations for Network Devices such as Firewalls, Routers, and Switches Critical Control 18: Incident Response and Management Critical Control 13: Boundary Defense
R3: Exceptions to the Cyber Security Policy	No Change	R3: Identify a CIP Senior Manager and document any change within 30 calendar days of the change	
R4: Information Protection Program	No Change	R4: CIP Senior Manager must document any delegates	
R5: Access Control	No Change		
R6: Change Control and Configuration Management	No Change		
CIP-004-3 Personnel and Training	**CIP-004-4 Personnel and Training**	**CIP-004-5 Personnel and Training**	
R1: Awareness: Security Awareness Program	No Change	R1: Security Awareness Program- reference Table 1: Security Awareness Program Criteria in standard	Critical Control 15: Controlled Access based on need to know Critical Control 9: Security Skills Assessment and appropriate training to fill gaps
R2: Training: Cyber Security Training Program	No Change	R2: Training Program- reference Table R2 Cyber Security Training Program in standard	Critical Control 15: Controlled Access based on need to know Critical Control 9: Security Skills Assessment and appropriate training to fill gaps
R3: Personnel Risk Assessment	No Change	R3: PRA Program- reference Table R3 PRA Program in standard	Critical Control 15: Controlled Access based on need to know Critical Control 9: Security Skills Assessment and appropriate training to fill gaps
R4: Access	No Change	R4: Access Management Program- Reference Table R4 Access Management Program in standard for required program criteria	Critical Control 15: Controlled Access based on need to know Critical Control 9: Security Skills Assessment and appropriate training to fill gaps
		R5: Access Revocation Program- Reference Table R5 Access Revocation for required program criteria	Critical Control 15: Controlled Access based on need to know Critical Control 9: Security Skills Assessment and appropriate training to fill gaps
CIP-005-3 Electronic Security Perimeter(s)	**CIP-005-4 Electronic Security Perimeter(s)**	**CIP-005-5 Electronic Security Perimeter(s)**	
R1: Electronic Security Perimeters: All CCAs must reside within an ESP	No Change	R1: Electronic Security Perimeters- reference Table R1 Electronic Security Perimeter for required criteria	Control 1: Inventory of Authorized and Unauthorized Devices Control 2: Inventory of Authorized and Unauthorized Software Control 4: Continuous Vulnerability Assessment and Remediation Critical Control 13: Boundary Defense
R2: Electronic Access Controls	No Change	R2: Interactive Remote Access Management Table R2	Control 1: Inventory of Authorized and Unauthorized Devices Control 2: Inventory of Authorized and Unauthorized Software Control 4: Continuous Vulnerability Assessment and Remediation Critical Control 13: Boundary Defense Critical Control 16: Account Monitoring and Control
R3: Monitoring Electronic Access	No Change		Control 1: Inventory of Authorized and Unauthorized Devices Control 2: Inventory of Authorized and Unauthorized Software Control 4: Continuous Vulnerability Assessment and Remediation Critical Control 13: Boundary Defense Critical Control 16: Account Monitoring and Control
R4: Cyber Vulnerability Assessment	No Change		Control 1: Inventory of Authorized and Unauthorized Devices Control 2: Inventory of Authorized and Unauthorized Software Control 4: Continuous Vulnerability Assessment and Remediation Critical Control 13: Boundary Defense Critical Control 16: Account Monitoring and Control
R5: Documentation Review and Maintenance	No Change		Control 1: Inventory of Authorized and Unauthorized Devices Control 2: Inventory of Authorized and Unauthorized Software Control 4: Continuous Vulnerability Assessment and Remediation Critical Control 13: Boundary Defense Critical Control 16: Account Monitoring and Control
CIP-006-3 Physical Security	**CIP-006-4 Physical Security**	**CIP-006-5 Physical Security of BES Cyber Systems**	
R1: Physical Security Plan	No Change	R1: Physical Security Plan table for criteria	Critical Control 9: Security Skills Assessment and Appropriate Training to fill gaps Critical Control 15: Controlled Access based on need to know Critical Control 13: Boundary Defense
R2: Protection of Physical Access Control Systems	No Change	R2: Visitor Control Plan- see table R2 Visitor Control Plan for criteria	Critical Control 9: Security Skills Assessment and Appropriate Training to fill gaps Critical Control 15: Controlled Access based on need to know Critical Control 13: Boundary Defense
R3: Protection of Electronic Access Control Systems	No Change	R3: Maintenance and Testing Program see table R3	Critical Control 9: Security Skills Assessment and Appropriate Training to fill gaps Critical Control 15: Controlled Access based on need to know Critical Control 13: Boundary Defense
R4: Physical Access Controls	No Change		Critical Control 9: Security Skills Assessment and Appropriate Training to fill gaps Critical Control 15: Controlled Access based on need to know Critical Control 13: Boundary Defense
R5: Monitoring Physical Access	No Change		Critical Control 9: Security Skills Assessment and Appropriate Training to fill gaps Critical Control 15: Controlled Access based on need to know Critical Control 13: Boundary Defense Critical Control 14: Maintenance, Monitoring and Analyis of Audit Logs
R6: Logging Physical Access	No Change		Critical Control 9: Security Skills Assessment and Appropriate Training to fill gaps Critical Control 15: Controlled Access based on need to know Critical Control 13: Boundary Defense Critical Control 14: Maintenance, Monitoring and Analyis of Audit Logs
R7: Access Log Retention	No Change		Critical Control 9: Security Skills Assessment and Appropriate Training to fill gaps Critical Control 15: Controlled Access based on need to know Critical Control 13: Boundary Defense Critical Control 14: Maintenance, Monitoring and Analyis of Audit Logs
R8: Maintenance and Testing	No Change		Critical Control 9: Security Skills Assessment and Appropriate Training to fill gaps Critical Control 15: Controlled Access based on need to know Critical Control 13: Boundary Defense Critical Control 14: Maintenance, Monitoring and Analyis of Audit Logs
CIP-007-3 Systems Security Management	**CIP-007-4 Systems Security Management**	**CIP-007-5 Systems Security Management**	
R1: Test Procedures	No Change	R1: Ports and Services See Table 1: Ports and Services in the standard for required criteria	Critical Control 13: Boundary Defense Critical Control 6: Application Software Security Critical Control 10: Secure Configurations for Network Devices such as Firewalls, routers and switches Critical Control 11: Limitation and Control of Network Ports, Protocols, and Services
R2: Ports and Services	No Change	R2: Security Patch Management Table R2 for required criteria	Critical Control 13: Boundary Defense Critical Control 6: Application Software Security Critical Control 10: Secure Configurations for Network Devices such as Firewalls, routers and switches Critical Control 11: Limitation and Control of Network Ports, Protocols, and Services
R3: Security Patch Management	No Change	R3: Malicious Code Prevention. See table R3 for required criteria	Critical Control 4: Continuous Vulnerability Assessment and remediation Critical Control 5: Malware Defenses Critical 6: Application Software Security Critical Control 20: Penetration Tests and Red Teaming
R4: Malicious Software Prevention	No Change	R4: Security Event Monitoring. See table R4 for required criteria	Critical Control 16: Account Monitoring and Control Critical Control 18: Incident Response and Management Critical Control 14: Maintenance, Monitoring, and Analysis of Audit Logs
R5: Account Management	No Change	R5: System Access Controls. See table R5 for required criteria	Critical Control 15: Controlled Access based on need to know Critical Control 19: Secure Network Engineering Critical Control 16: Account Monitoring and Control
R6: Security Status Monitoring	No Change		Critical Control 16: Account Monitoring and Control Critical Control 18: Incident Response and Management Critical Control 14: Maintenance, Monitoring, and Analysis of Audit Logs
R7: Disposal or Redeployment	No Change		Critical Control 8: Data Recovery Capability
R8: Cyber Vulnerability Assessment	No Change		Critical Control 4: Continuous Vulnerability Assessment and Remediation
R9: Documentation Review and Maintenance	No Change		
CIP-008-3 Incident Reporting and Response Planning	**CIP-008-4 Incident Reporting and Response Planning**	**CIP-008-5 Incident Reporting and Response Planning**	
R1: Cyber Security Incident Response Plan	No Change	R1: Cyber Security Incident Response Plan	Critical Control 18: Incident Response and Management
R2: Cyber Security Incident Documentation	No Change	R2: Implementation and testing of Cyber Security Incident Response Plans	Critical Control 18: Incident Response and Management
		R3: Cyber Security Incident Response Plan Review, Update and Communication	Critical Control 18: Incident Response and Management
CIP-009-3 Recovery Plans for Critical Cyber Assets	**CIP-009-4 Recovery Plans for Critical Cyber Assets**	**CIP-009-5 Recovery Plans for BES Cyber Systems**	
R1: Recovery Plans	No Change	Recovery Plan Specifications see table R1	Critical Control 17: Data Loss Prevention Critical Control 18: Incident Response and Management Critical Control 8: Data Recovery Capability
R2: Exercises	No Change	Recovery Plan Implementation and Testing see table R2	Critical Control 17: Data Loss Prevention Critical Control 18: Incident Response and Management Critical Control 8: Data Recovery Capability
R3: Change Control	No Change	Recovery Plan review, udpate and communication	Critical Control 1: Inventory of Authorized and Unauthorized devices Critical Control 2: Inventory of Authorized and Unauthorized Software Critical Control 8: Data Recovery Capability
R4: Backup and Restore	No Change		Critical Control 1: Inventory of Authorized and Unauthorized devices Critical Control 2: Inventory of Authorized and Unauthorized Software Critical Control 8: Data Recovery Capability
R5: Testing Back Up Media	No Change		Critical Control 1: Inventory of Authorized and Unauthorized devices Critical Control 2: Inventory of Authorized and Unauthorized Software Critical Control 8: Data Recovery Capability
		CIP-010-1 Configuration Change Management and Vulnerability Assessments	Critical Control 1: Inventory of Authorized and Unauthorized devices Critical Control 2: Inventory of Authorized and Unauthorized Software Critical Control 8: Data Recovery Capability
		R1: Configuration Change Management Process see table R1	Critical Control 1: Inventory of Authorized and Unauthorized devices Critical Control 2: Inventory of Authorized and Unauthorized Software Critical Control 8: Data Recovery Capability
		R2: Configuration Monitoring see table R2	Critical Control 1: Inventory of Authorized and Unauthorized devices Critical Control 2: Inventory of Authorized and Unauthorized Software Critical Control 8: Data Recovery Capability
		R3: Vulnerability Assessments Table R3	Critical Control 1: Inventory of Authorized and Unauthorized devices Critical Control 2: Inventory of Authorized and Unauthorized Software Critical Control 8: Data Recovery Capability
		CIP-011-1 Information Protection	Critical Control 1: Inventory of Authorized and Unauthorized devices Critical Control 2: Inventory of Authorized and Unauthorized Software Critical Control 8: Data Recovery Capability
		R1: Information Protection Process- see table R1	Critical Control 1: Inventory of Authorized and Unauthorized devices Critical Control 2: Inventory of Authorized and Unauthorized Software Critical Control 8: Data Recovery Capability
		R2: BES Cyber Asset Reuse and Disposal	Critical Control 1: Inventory of Authorized and Unauthorized devices Critical Control 2: Inventory of Authorized and Unauthorized Software Critical Control 8: Data Recovery Capability

© The SANS Institute & The Anfield Group 2013

Figure 6.2: Evolution of NERC CIP Standards showing an evolution toward consideration of devices as the boundary. From [9], Copyright 2003.

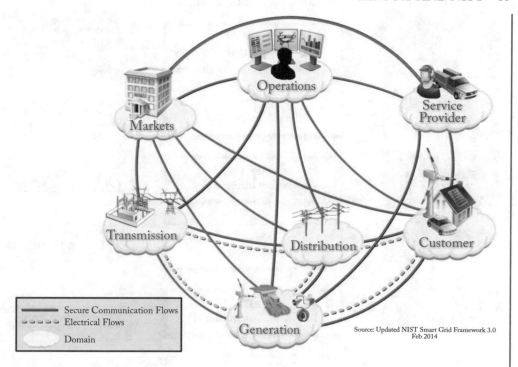

Figure 6.3: Domains enumerated by NISTIR 7628 [11].

lated to the AMI environment. In volume 2, rather than being concerned about interception of meter data, of particular privacy interest are the potential for privacy violations in collecting meter data. The primary concern is that the electric utility might sell such data to a third party. The privacy approach is taken from an auditing point of view with respect to the risks involved. The document concludes with future directions for dealing with non-centralized control and management and customer-owned equipment; this discussion continues within the NIST Public Working Group (PWG) on CPS [10] and in the openFMB effort.

6.2.2   NIST 800-030

The "Guide for Conducting Risk Assessments" [7] is not specifically for cybersecurity, but its methodology finds a natural home in the multiple security domain environment of a smart grid (see Figure 6.4).

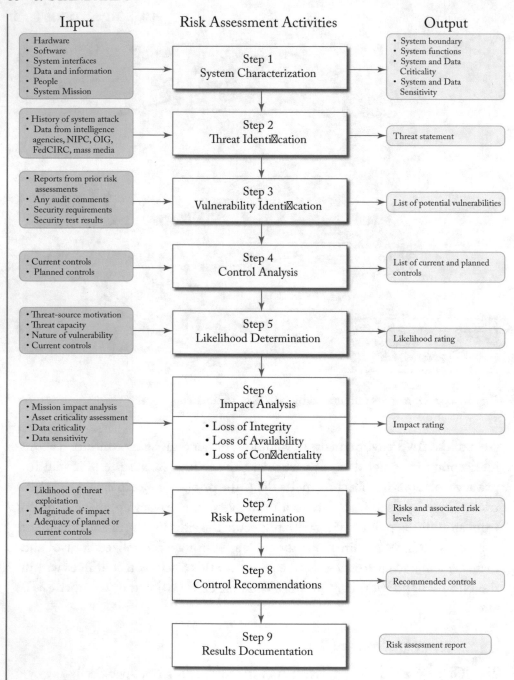

Figure 6.4: NIST 800-30 Risk Assessment Methodology where the first step is to draw the boundaries of the system [7].

6.2.3 OPENFMB

openFMB [13] is an effort largely led by Duke Energy to "define a reference architecture platform comprising internet protocol (IP) networking, Internet of Things (IoT) messaging protocols, standardized common semantic models, messages, and services to enable the secure, reliable, and scalable communications and peer-to-peer information exchange between devices on the electric grid." The principal effort, as of this writing, has been to develop communications use cases.

The key long-term contribution of openFMB will be to develop distributed IoT interaction protocols for management of electric power systems that moves away from centralized management and control into a peer-to-peer reconfigurable architecture. Working with North American Energy Standards Board (NAESB) will potentially provide openFMB as a standard. It remains an open question as to whether openFMB will complement or compete with similar standards activities, such as IEC 61850 for substation automation.

Security within openFMB is limited to processing of a "security event" [15]. Little else is said within the standard of how this is detected, and the openFMB standard refers to other best practices for security. Practically, at the time of this writing, asymmetric key exchange and trust among openFMB components is the principal defense.

6.2.4 MANDATE M/441, CG-SM, AND SGAM

The European Commission mandate M/441 creates a number of standards to enable interoperability of utility meters to improve the customer's awareness of their actual consumption. The Smart Meters Coordination Group (CG-SM) produced the Smart Grid Architecture Model (SGAM)in terms of communications standards, interoperability, and relationship with the business enterprise in terms of layers and planes [2].

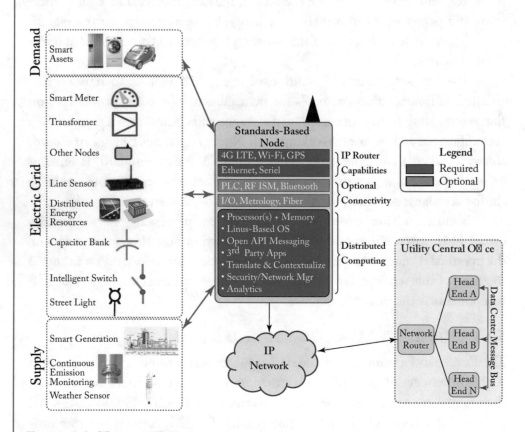

Figure 6.5: The openFMB node that provides interoperability among disparate devices [13].

CHAPTER 7

Summary

This book has concentrated on uncovering the limitations of existing security models and methods in evolving smart grid architectures. Key is the notion of understanding information flow among the various components, cyber, power, communications, and inhabitants. Current thoughts in terms of improving defenses and policies are given in each section. There is an inertia in industrial movement; utilities and smart grid providers are in compliance with standards. Moving forward, standards must evolve away from the existing top-down SCADA-like structures and understand that current notions of trust are inadequate in evolving internet of energy environments.

Bibliography

[1] Technical report, National Science Foundation, Cyber-physical Systems Program. http://www.nist.gov/cps/ 1

[2] European Commission Mandate M/441. http://www.etsi.org/tec hnologies-clusters/technologies/internet-of-things/smart-metering, accessed 7/1/2017. 37

[3] IPERC Corporate Website. http://iperc.com, accessed 7/1/2017. 3

[4] ISO/IEC Information Security Management Systems (ISMS) standards. http://www.27000.org/index.htm, accessed 7/1/2017. 7

[5] Technical analysis of the August 14, 2003, blackout: What happened, why, and what did we learn? https://reports.energy.gov/BlackoutF inal-Web.pdf, accessed January 20, 2016. Technical report. 31

[6] Technical report, National Institute of Standards and Technology. http://sgip.org/NISTIR-7628-User-s-Guide---Smart-Grid-Cyber-Security-Implementation-Guidelines 32

[7] Guide for Conducting Risk Assessments. Technical report, NIST, 2012. 25, 35, 36

[8] *Terrorism and the Electric Power Delivery System.* National Academies Press, 2012. DOI: 10.17226/12050. 8, 9, 25

[9] Technical report, SANS Institute. https://www.sans.org/.../nerc-cip-mapping-sans20-csc.pdf 34

[10] Technical report, National Institute of Standards and Technology. http://www.nist.gov/cps/cpspwg.cfm 1, 35

[11] Technical report, National Institute of Standards and Technology. http://nvlpubs.nist.gov/nistpubs/ir/2014/NIST.IR.7628r1.pdf 28, 32, 35

[12] Technical report, North American Electric Reliability Corporation (NERC). http://www.nerc.com/pa/Stand/Pages/CIPStandards.asp x 19, 33

[13] Technical report, Smart Grid Interoperability Panel, Open Field Message Bus Standard Draft. http://members.sgip.org/apps/org/workgrou p/ofmb/download.php/7238/retail_open_fmb092515a1.docx 37, 38

[14] Cyber security task force action plan. Technical report, State of Missouri, December 2016. 25

[15] Technical report, NAESB Open Field Message Bus (OpenFMB) Model Business Practices—RMQ.26, available from North American Energy Standards Board. https://www.naesb.org//pdf/ordrform.pdf 37

[16] NIST Cybersecurity Practice Guide, SP 1800-7 Situational Awareness for Electric Utilities. Technical report, NIST, 2017. 25

[17] R. Akella, F. Meng, D. Ditch, B. McMillin, and M. Crow. Distributed power balancing for the freedom system. In *Smart Grid Communications (SmartGridComm), 1st IEEE International Conference on*, pages 7–12, October 2010. DOI: 10.1109/smartgrid.2010.5622003. 3

[18] M. Bishop. *Computer Security: Art and Science*. Addison-Wesley Longman Publishing Co., Inc., Boston, MA, 2002. 10, 12

[19] R. B. Bobba, K. M. Rogers, Q. Wang, H. Khurana, K. Nahrstedt, and T. J. Overbye. Detecting false data injection attacks on DC state estimation. In *Preprints of the 1st Workshop on Secure Control Systems, CPSWEEK*, volume 2010, 2010. 21

[20] A. Bose and K. Tomsovic. *Wiley Encyclopedia of Electrical and Electronics Engineering*, chapter Power System Security, 1999. xi

[21] L. Briesemeister, S. Cheung, U. Lindqvist, and A. Valdes. Detection, correlation, and visualization of attacks against critical infrastructure systems. In *Privacy Security and Trust (PST), 8th Annual International Conference on*, pages 15–22, August 2010. DOI: 10.1109/pst.2010.5593242. 18

[22] A. A. Cardenas, S. Amin, Z.-S. Lin, Y.-L. Huang, C.-Y. Huang, and S. Sastry. Attacks against process control systems: Risk assessment, detection, and response. In *Proc. of the 6th ACM Symposium on Information, Computer and Communications Security*, pages 355–366, 2011. DOI: 10.1145/1966913.1966959. 23

[23] C. M. Chiappetta and C. B. Brown. Nuclear plant security: Plant physical design features. *Power Apparatus and Systems, IEEE Transactions on*, 96(1):52–58, January 1977. DOI: 10.1109/t-pas.1977.32306. 8

[24] B. J. Cory. An approach by means of mathematical logic to the switching of power system networks. *Proc. IEE(London)*, 110(1):185, 1963. DOI: 10.1049/piee.1963.0026. 8

[25] M. Couvreur. Logic-adaptive process for control and security in interconnected power systems. *Power Apparatus and Systems, IEEE Transactions on*, PAS-87(12):1979–1985, December 1968. DOI: 10.1109/tpas.1968.292157. 8

[26] G. Dán and H. Sandberg. Stealth attacks and protection schemes for state estimators in power systems. In *Smart Grid Communications (SmartGridComm), 1st IEEE International Conference on*, pages 214–219, 2010. DOI: 10.1109/smartgrid.2010.5622046. 21

[27] N. Falliere, L. O. Murchu, and E. Chien. W32. Stuxnet dossier. *White Paper, Symantec Corp., Security Response*, 2011. 15

[28] A. Faza, S. Sedigh, and B. McMillin. Reliability analysis for the advanced electric power grid: From cyber control and communication to physical manifestations of failure. In *Proc. of the International Conference on Computer Safety, Reliability and Security (SAFECOMP'09)*, pages 257–269, best paper award, September 2009. DOI: 10.1007/978-3-642-04468-7_21. 19

[29] T. T. Gamage, T. P. Roth, B. M. McMillin, and M. L. Crow. Mitigating event confidentiality violations in smart grids: An information flow security-based approach. *Smart Grid, IEEE Transactions on*, 4(3):1227–1234, 2013. DOI: 10.1109/tsg.2013.2243924. 19

[30] J. A. Goguen and J. Meseguer. Security policies and security models. In *Symposium on Security and Privacy*, pages 11–20, Oakland, CA, IEEE Computer Society, April 1982. DOI: 10.1109/sp.1982.10014. 16

[31] M. Harvey, D. Long, and K. Reinhard. Visualizing NISTIR 7628, guidelines for smart grid cyber security. In *Power and Energy Conference at Illinois (PECI)*, pages 1–8, February 2014. DOI: 10.1109/peci.2014.6804566. 32

[32] D. He, W. Lin, N. Liu, R. G. Harley, and T. G. Habetler. Incorporating non-intrusive load monitoring into building level demand response. *IEEE Transactions on Smart Grid*, 4(4):1870–1877, December 2013. DOI: 10.1109/tsg.2013.2258180. 27

[33] C. T. T. Ho, R. Yan, T. K. Saha, and S. E. Goodwin. Design microgrid for a distribution network: A case study of the university of queensland. In *Power and Energy Society General Meeting (PES)*, pages 1–5, IEEE, July 2013. DOI: 10.1109/pesmg.2013.6672192. 1

[34] J. Hong, C.-C. Liu, and M. Govindarasu. Integrated anomaly detection for cyber security of the substations. *Smart Grid, IEEE Transactions on*, 5(4):1643–1653, July 2014. DOI: 10.1109/tsg.2013.2294473. 18

[35] G. S. Hope and B. J. Cory. Development of digital computer programs for the automatic switching of power networks. *Power Apparatus and Systems, IEEE Transactions on*, PAS-87(7):1587–1599, July 1968. DOI: 10.1109/tpas.1968.292245. 8

[36] G. Howser and B. McMillin. A modal model of stuxnet attacks on cyber-physical systems: A matter of trust. In *Software Security and Reliability (SERE), 8th International Conference on*, pages 225–234, June 2014. DOI: 10.1109/sere.2014.36. 16

[37] G. Howser and B. McMillin. Using information-flow methods to analyze the security of cyber-physical systems. *Computer*, 50(4):17–26, April 2017. DOI: 10.1109/mc.2017.112. 16

[38] Industrial Control Systems Cyber Emergency Response Team. Standards and References. Technical report, Department of Homeland Security. 10

[39] F. Khorrami, P. Krishnamurthy, and R. Karri. Cybersecurity for control systems: A process-aware perspective. *IEEE Design Test*, 33(5):75–83, October 2016. DOI: 10.1109/mdat.2016.2594178. 22

[40] C. Kil, E. C. Sezer, A. M. Azab, P. Ning, and X. Zhang. Remote attestation to dynamic system properties: Towards providing complete system integrity evidence. In *Dependable Systems Networks, DSN'09, IEEE/IFIP International Conference on*, pages 115–124, June 2009. DOI: 10.1109/dsn.2009.5270348. 21

[41] J. Kim and L. Tong. On topology attack of a smart grid: Undetectable attacks and countermeasures. *Selected Areas in Communications, IEEE Journal on*, 31(7):1294–1305, 2013. DOI: 10.1109/jsac.2013.130712. 20

[42] L. Lamport, R. Shostak, and M. Pease. The byzantine generals problem. *ACM Transactions on Programming Languages Systems*, 4(3):382–401, July 1982. DOI: 10.1145/357172.357176. 23

[43] R. M. Lee, M. J. Assante, and T. Conway. Analysis of the Cyber Attack on the Ukrainian Power Grid. Technical report, SANS Industrial Control Systems and E-ISAC—The Electricity Information Sharing and Analysis Center, March 2016. 25

[44] J. Lin, W. Yu, X. Yang, G. Xu, and W. Zhao. On false data injection attacks against distributed energy routing in smart grid. In *Cyber-physical Systems (ICCPS), IEEE/ACM 3rd International Conference on*, pages 183–192, 2012. DOI: 10.1109/iccps.2012.26. 22

[45] Y. Liu, P. Ning, and M. K Reiter. False data injection attacks against state estimation in electric power grids. *ACM Transactions on Information and System Security (TISSEC)*, 14(1):13, 2011. DOI: 10.1145/1952982.1952995. 20

[46] B. McMillin, R. Akella, D. Ditch, G. Heydt, Z. Zhang, and M.-Y. Chow. Architecture of a smart microgrid distributed operating system. In *Power Systems Conference and Exposition (PSCE), IEEE/PES*, pages 1–5, March 2011. DOI: 10.1109/psce.2011.5772496. 1, 3

[47] J. A. Mueller, A. Sankara, J. W. Kimball, and B. McMillin. Hidden Markov models for nonintrusive appliance load monitoring. In *North*

American Power Symposium (NAPS), pages 1–6, September 2014. DOI: 10.1109/naps.2014.6965464. 27

[48] M. Nabeel, S. Kerr, X. Ding, and E. Bertino.   Authentication and key management for advanced metering infrastructures utilizing physically unclonable functions.   In *IEEE 3rd International Conference on Smart Grid Communications (SmartGridComm)*, pages 324–329, November 2012. DOI: 10.1109/smartgridcomm.2012.6486004. 22

[49] T. D. Nicol and D. M. Nicol.   Combating unauthorized load signal analysis with targeted event masking.   In *System Science (HICSS), 45th Hawaii International Conference on*, pages 2037–2043, January 2012. DOI: 10.1109/hicss.2012.161. 27

[50] Office of Electric Energy Delivery and Energy Reliability.   21 Steps to Improve Cyber Security of SCADA Networks.   Technical report, U.S. Department of Energy, 2002. 8

[51] H. Park, D. Seo, H. Lee, and A. Perrig.   SMATT: Smart meter attestation using multiple target selection and copy-proof memory.   In *Computer Science and its Applications*, pages 875–887, Springer, 2012. DOI: 10.1007/978-94-007-5699-1_90. 22

[52] A. M. Pasdar, Y. Sozer, and I. Husain. Detecting and locating faulty nodes in smart grids based on high frequency signal injection. *Smart Grid, IEEE Transactions on*, 4(2):1067–1075, 2013. DOI: 10.1109/tsg.2012.2221148. 15

[53] S. Petronio. *Boundaries of Privacy: Dialectics of Disclosure*. SUNY Press, 2012. 29

[54] O. Pradhan, M. Awan, K. Newman, and F. Barnes. Trust and reputation approach to smart grid security. In *Resilient Control Systems (IS-RCS), 4th International Symposium on*, pages 101–104, August 2011. DOI: 10.1109/isrcs.2011.6016097. 23

[55] T. Roth and B. McMillin. Physical attestation of cyber processes in the smart grid. In *Critical Information Infrastructures Security*, pages 96–107, Springer, 2013. DOI: 10.1007/978-3-319-03964-0_9. 21, 23

[56] J. Rrushi and K.-D. Kang. Detecting anomalies in process control networks. In C. Palmer and S. Shenoi, Eds., *Critical Infrastructure Protection III*, volume 311 of *IFIP Advances in Information and Communication Technology*, pages 151–165, Springer Berlin Heidelberg, 2009. DOI: 10.1007/978-3-642-04798-5. 23

[57] H. Sandberg, A. Teixeira, and K. H. Johansson. On security indices for state estimators in power networks. In *1st Workshop on Secure Control Systems (SCS)*, Stockholm, 2010. 21

[58] F. C. Schweppe. Power system static-state estimation, part III: Implementation. *Power Apparatus and Systems, IEEE Transactions on*, PAS-89(1):130–135, January 1970. DOI: 10.1109/tpas.1970.292680. 20

[59] A. Seshadri, M. Luk, E. Shi, A. Perrig, L. van Doorn, and P. Khosla. Pioneer: Verifying code integrity and enforcing untampered code execution on legacy systems. In *Proc. of the 20th ACM Symposium on Operating Systems Principles, SOSP'05*, pages 1–16, New York, 2005. DOI: 10.1145/1095810.1095812. 21

[60] A. Seshadri, A. Perrig, L. van Doorn, and P. Khosla. SWATT: Software-based attestation for embedded devices. In *Proc. of the Security and Privacy, IEEE Symposium on*, pages 272–282, 2004. DOI: 10.1109/secpri.2004.1301329. 21

[61] M. Shaneck, K. Mahadevan, V. Kher, and Y. Kim. Remote software-based attestation for wireless sensors. In R. Molva, G. Tsudik, and D. Westhoff, Eds., *Security and Privacy in Ad-hoc and Sensor Networks*, volume 3813 of *Lecture Notes in Computer Science*, pages 27–41, Springer Berlin Heidelberg, 2005. DOI: 10.1007/11601494. 21

[62] S. R. Shaw, S. B. Leeb, L. K. Norford, and R. W. Cox. Nonintrusive load monitoring and diagnostics in power systems. 57(7):1445–1454, July 2008. DOI: 10.1109/tim.2008.917179. 27

[63] T. Sommestad, G. N. Ericsson, and J. Nordlander. Scada system cyber security #x2014; a comparison of standards. In *Power and Energy Society General Meeting, IEEE*, pages 1–8, July 2010. DOI: 10.1109/pes.2010.5590215. 10

[64] K. Song, D. Seo, H. Park, H. Lee, and A. Perrig. OMAP: One-way memory attestation protocol for smart meters. In *Parallel and Distributed Processing with Applications Workshops (ISPAW), 9th IEEE International Symposium on*, pages 111–118, 2011. DOI: 10.1109/ispaw.2011.37. 22

[65] K. C. Sou, H. Sandberg, and K. H. Johansson. Data attack isolation in power networks using secure voltage magnitude measurements. *Smart Grid, IEEE Transactions on*, 5(1):14–28, 2014. DOI: 10.1109/tsg.2013.2280658. 22

[66] D. Sutherland. A model of information. In *Proc. 9th National Computer Security Conference*, pages 175–183, DTIC Document, 1986. 15

[67] A. Tajer, S. Kar, H. V. Poor, and S. Cui. Distributed joint cyber attack detection and state recovery in smart grids. In *Smart Grid Communications (SmartGridComm), IEEE International Conference on*, pages 202–207, 2011. DOI: 10.1109/smartgridcomm.2011.6102319. 22

[68] C.-W. Ten, C.-C. Liu, and G. Manimaran. Vulnerability assessment of cybersecurity for scada systems. *Power Systems, IEEE Transactions on*, 23(4):1836–1846, November 2008. DOI: 10.1109/pes.2007.385876. 18

[69] J. Valente, C. Barreto, and A. A. Cárdenas. Cyber-physical systems attestation. In *Distributed Computing in Sensor Systems (DCOSS), IEEE International Conference on*, pages 354–357, 2014. DOI: 10.1109/dcoss.2014.61. 21, 22

[70] Z. Wang and G. Zheng. Residential appliances identification and monitoring by a nonintrusive method. *IEEE Transactions on Smart Grid*, 3(1):80–92, March 2012. DOI: 10.1109/tsg.2011.2163950. 27

[71] L. Xie, Y. Mo, and B. Sinopoli. Integrity data attacks in power market operations. *Smart Grid, IEEE Transactions on*, 2(4):659–666, 2011. DOI: 10.1109/tsg.2011.2161892. 25

[72] S. Xin, Q. Guo, H. Sun, B. Zhang, J. Wang, and C. Chen. Cyber-physical modeling and cyber-contingency assessment of hierarchical control systems. *Smart Grid, IEEE Transactions on*, 6(5):2375–2385, September 2015. DOI: 10.1109/tsg.2014.2387381. 7, 19

[73] M. Zeifman and K. Roth. Nonintrusive appliance load monitoring: Review and outlook. *Proc. of the IEEE*, 57(1):76–84, February 2011. DOI: 10.1109/icce.2011.5722560. 23, 27

[74] W. Zeng, Y. Zhang, and M. Chow. A resilient distributed energy management algorithm for economic dispatch in the presence of misbehaving generation units. In *Resilience Week (RWS)*, pages 1–5, August 2015. DOI: 10.1109/rweek.2015.7287411. 23

[75] Y. Zhang, L. Wang, Y. Xiang, and C.-W. Ten. Power system reliability evaluation with scada cybersecurity considerations. *Smart Grid, IEEE Transactions on*, 6(4):1707–1721, July 2015. DOI: 10.1109/tsg.2015.2396994. 18

Authors' Biographies

BRUCE MCMILLIN

 **Dr. Bruce McMillin** is currently a Professor of Computer Science, Associate Dean of Engineering and Computing, director of the Center for Information Assurance, co-director of the Center for Smart Living, and a senior research investigator in the Intelligent Systems Center all at the Missouri University of Science and Technology. He leads and participates in interdisciplinary teams in formal methods for fault tolerance and security in distributed embedded systems with an eye towards critical infrastructure protection. His current work focuses on protection for advanced power grid control. His research has been supported by the United States NSF, AFOSR, DOE, NIST, and several Missouri Industries. Dr. McMillin has authored over 100 refereed papers in international conferences and journals. He is leading the distributed grid intelligence project of the Future Renewables NSF Engineering Research Center, an advanced smart grid architecture. He is a senior member of the IEEE and member of the IFIP WG 11.0 on Critical Infrastructure Protection, and member and contributor to the SGIP Smart Grid Interoperability Panel. He currently serves in the IEEE Computer Society's Board of Governors and is a member of the Computing ABET Accreditation Commission.

THOMAS ROTH

Thomas Roth received his Ph.D. in Computer Science from Missouri University of Science and Technology in 2015. He now works at the National Institute of Standards and Technology as part of its Smart Grid and Cyber Physical Systems Program Office. His research interests are in information flow security and the detection of compromised processes in distributed cyberphysical systems.